The Art of Making Wax Leaves

Anna M. Hyde

ISBN 978-1-300-26131-5
90000
9 781300 261315

THE ART

OF

Making Wax Leaves,

BY

MRS. A. M. HYDE.

PUBLISHED BY

JANENTZKY & CO., 1125 CHESTNUT STREET,

PHILADELPHIA.

THE ART OF

Making Wax Leaves.

Of all the various artistic uses to which sheet wax is applied, perhaps none is more effective or more closely imitative of nature than the manufacture of leaves. Autumnal tints in all their gorgeous variety and blended hues, green ferns and white veined ivy, and—most striking of all—the rare foliaged exotics seen in hot-house collections,—Colladiums, Bigonias, Coleus, Cissus discolor, and many others. We do not now allude to the many miserable specimens seen in shop windows and arranged in vases upon mantel shelves, to be admired only by the makers themselves or by those who have never seen the natural leaves of which they are supposed to be copies. Such efforts as these do not deserve the name, and would disgust the taste-

ful amateur, and deter him from attempting the art. The simple directions we are about to give will enable any one to produce specimens of quite another type, which will amply reward the small outlay of time and capital required for their manufacture.

For Autumn leaves, use white wax for all variegated or red ones, but yellow wax will be best for the yellow tinted varieties. Use patterns taken from natural leaves, and with a pair of small scissors cut them neatly out of the wax, using for the purpose two sheets pressed firmly together. Some persons cut the sheets separately and press them together afterwards, but this is double trouble, as they can just as well be cut at once, and the stem—a wire covered with wax—can be easily inserted between the two thicknesses, letting it extend along the centre almost to the point of the leaf, like the mid-rib of a natural leaf. If maple leaves are to be made, they can be moulded around the edges by pressing them firmly with the ball of the moulding pin, the edge of the leaf being held over the forefinger of the left hand. Then, holding the leaf in the palm of

your left hand, begin to mould it from the central stem outwards, until the two sheets of wax are completely incorporated together.

Next; wet the right side of the leaf—the side that has been held next the palm, and press it down firmly upon the natural leaf, which will thus impart the proper impressions of veins, and also the natural bend of the leaf itself.

Next comes the coloring, which is no unimportant matter, and will need some practice before producing the right effect. Perhaps it will be best for a beginner to try blending the tints first upon a piece of waste wax. Rub a small portion of the carmine upon a portion of it and shade it on the edges with black or brown, until the easy art is acquired.

Some of the prettiest of the maples are of three distinct colors, yellow, red and green. One point will be of the clearest crimson, deepening in places into a purplish brown; another will be yellow, shaded into orange and brown, and in another portion will be seen the natural green, perhaps spotted and marked by insects, but blending and changing very gradu-

ally into the other colors. In the imitation of this easy blending of shades consists the chief art of the coloring.

Take powder colors, prepared for wax work, —chrome green, chrome yellow, carmine, and a little vandyke brown. The green will need a little of the yellow added to make it of the natural tint. With one of the middle fingers, rub on the green powder on both sides of a portion of the leaf, working it well into the veins and edges. Next rub pine yellow into another part, and then upon a third the carmine; then let the parts where the colors meet be shaded together, adding enough brown or ivory black to darken and shade it wherever it is desirable.

In the same way may be colored any of the autumn tinted leaves, nature furnishing enough brilliant specimens from which to copy. If any of the more sombre or russet tinted leaves are wanted to mix in the gay group, they may be colored with raw sienna, brightened, pĕrhaps, by adding a little touch of burnt sienna to the edges.

Other leaves, however, will require different

treatment. Coleus leaves should be made of light green wax, and moulded upon regular moulds, either of plaster or metal, to be had of various sizes at the places where other materials for wax work are sold.

When made and moulded, the color, composed of carmine and vandyke brown well mixed, is rubbed upon the central portion, and may be made to imitate nature very closely, especially when the edges are left clear and green. Or if green wax is not at hand, white will answer very well by merely rubbing light green paint on to the edges before putting on the color for the centre. The less it is rubbed the more velvety will be the appearance of the leaf. Leaves of the Virginia creeper, and sumac are of a very brilliant red color; sweet gum, blackberry, sassafras, etc., are of variegated hues.

The exotic foliaged plants, which have been but lately introduced into our gardens and hot houses, are capable of the closest imitation, but are colored in a different manner. Oil colors in tubes are used for them, and also dry zinc white, where a peculiar kind of white is desired. For

Calladiums, of which there are quite a variety, a different method of moulding must be observed. For the dark green species use wax of the natural shades; cut them out of three thicknesses of what is called single wax, or two of the double, always proceeding, if possible, with a natural leaf as the model. Mould the wax leaf with three or five wires instead of one; let one mark the centre, and two others curve from the two barbed points of the arrow-shaped leaf, the remaining two starting from points nearer the apex and uniting with the central wire, forming one stem at the base of the leaf. (*See illustration*).

A plaster mould will afford both a pattern of form and a means of giving it shape and roundness. Of the green Calladiums some are marked with red or pinkish blotches, which can be given with sable brushes, using crimson lake with a little white to give it body; for white marks use the silver or cremnitz white, and for lighter green, add chrome green toned to the proper shade by adding white or chrome yellow, or perhaps some of both.

For all veined leaves use a very finely pointed

sable pencil and cremnitz white, tracing them firmly but lightly along the lines indicated by the mould.

For the white *Calladium* or rather the light green and white variety, use white wax, rendered still whiter by rubbing with zinc white in powder. These leaves are curiously marked and mottled with green, and this mottling is given by applying to the edges, and different portions of the leaf, touches of green paint mixed to the proper tint. After it has been applied in a rough and seemingly careless manner, take a badger blender and pass it back and forth across, and up and down the leaf, until the proper blending mottling is attained.

The leaves of the *Cissus discolor* are very curiously spotted with light green beads upon a ground of dark green and purplish crimson. Mould the leaves as usual upon moulds made of different sizes, and commence by painting the leaves with crimson lake; this will give the veins the peculiar purplish tint seen in these leaves. When dry, the spots are to be given with naples yellow paint, slightly tinted with green, imitating nature in the shape and size of the spots.

Another plant, very well worth copying in wax, is the *Achyranthus* with its crimson and dark brown leaves, looking so brilliant in the sunlight. Plaster moulds in various sizes and shapes are needed for these peculiar looking leaves. Some of the leaves are only half open, others drawn down in the centre, whilst others will be fully expanded, and the full variety is necessary to the perfect representation. A wire through the centre, as with ordinary leaves, will be sufficient for any of them, and it can be bent to suit the shape of the mould. Use white wax, and after all are moulded begin by painting them entirely on both sides and the stem with crimson lake, putting them carefully by to dry. If the color is not as deep as in the natural leaves, give a second coat, which will produce a fine clear crimson or blood color. When this is dry enough mark the lines or stripes with vandyke brown, and leave them to dry.

For the leaves of Begonias, use white wax of three thicknesses, mould and paint the edges with dull green made by mixing chrome green, naples yellow and a little vandyke brown; then paint the centre of a lighter shade, produced by

adding white to the same. The under side of the leaf must be washed with crimson lake, with a slight addition of vandyke brown to give it body.

In addition to the above-named varieties, there are many other curiously marked leaves which may be colored in oils, but the above directions will afford sufficient guide to them, and by closely imitating the natural leaves themselves, learners will readily acquire the art.

SHEET WAX*—Best Quality in the Market.*—White, Green, Yellow, Blue, Pink, Purple, Buff—for Tea Rose, Browns—for autumn leaves, Orange, Variegated—plain, Scarlet, Crimson, White—double, Variegated—with Carmine.

EXTRA LARGE WAX*—For Pond Lilies, in Packages of 6 Sheets.*—White, Green, assorted.

WHITE CAKE WAX*—Warranted Pure.*—The celebrated "Star Brand."

EXTRA FINE DRY COLORS*—In small glass bottles. prepared expressly for this work and for Initial Stamping.*—White, Burnt Sienna. Burnt Umber, Raw Umber, Raw Sienna, Chrome Yellow—Nos 1. 2, Chrome Orange, Light Blue, Prussian Blue, Green—light, medium, dark, Yellow Ochre, Indian Red, Light Red, Lamp Black. Down—in different tints, Rose, Deep Rose, Purple, Solferino, Bloom. Magenta. Vermillion. Frosting—white and colored, Lemon Yellow, Pure Scarlet, Cobalt, Carmine—small and large size vials. Violet Carmine. Fine Dry Colors, fitted in boxes. an assortment of 28 different Colors, complete for use.

GILT LEAF MOULDS—Violet, Nos. 1, 2, 3. Camelia. 4, 5. Fuchsia, 6, 7, 8. Fish Geranium, 9, 17, 18. Ivy, 10, 11, 35. Rose, 12, 13, 14. 22, 34. 68, 69. Lily of Valley, 15, 16. Verbena, 19, 20, 21. Orange, 23. 24. Heliotrope, 25. 26, 27. Arbutilon, 28, 29. Pansey, 30, 31. Rose Geranium, 32. 33. Pond Lily, 36. 37. Maple, 38, 39, 40, 41. Oak, 42, 43, 44. Dog Wood, 45, 46 Chestnut, 47, 48. Sassafras, 49, 49½, 50. Blackbery, 51, 52, 53. Elm, 54, 55. Sumac, 56, 57. Wild Cherry, 59, 58, 58½. Grape, 60, 61. Currant, 62, 63. Jessamine, 64, 65. Willow, 66, 67. Butterfly, 71, 72, 73. Myrtle, 74, 75, 76. Cape Jessamine, Salvia, Honey Suckle, Laurustinus, Azalia, Lilac, Strawberry, Pyrus Japonica, Clemestine, Woodbine, Passion Flower.

GILT FLOWER CUTTERS*—Extra Fine of 1 piece each.*—Verbena, 77, 78, 79. Heliotrope and Forget Me Not, 80, 81.

TIN FLOWER CUTTERS—Dahlia. 7 pieces, No. 1. Camelia, 6 pieces, 2. Rose, 8 pieces. 3. Fuchsia, 2 pieces, 4. Geranium, 3 pieces, 6. Lily of Valley, 7. Violet, 2 pieces, 10. Wisteria, 3 pieces, 13. Pyrus Japonica. 2 pieces, 14. Honeysuckle, 15. Pink, 4 pieces. 16. Pansey, 4 pieces, 17. Geranium, 18. Jessamine. 19. Orange, 20. Pond Lily, 8 pieces, 21. Tube Rose, 4 pieces, 22. Sweet Alysium, 23. Moss Rose Calyx, 24. Clemestine or small Jessamine, 25. Star Flower, 26. Quaker Lady, 27. Azalia, Nos. 31, 32, 33. Easter Lily, 34, Narcissus, 35.

SUNDRIES—Carmine Saucers. Green Moss, in Envelopes, in fine sprigs. Staminas, a great variety. Wooden Crosses, painted white, 6, 7, 8½, 9½. 10½, 12, 14, 16 and 18 inches high. Rustic Crosses, neatly made, of different sizes. Cross, Heart and Anchor, nicely arranged to represent Faith, Hope and Charity. Harps. Lyres. Anchors. Megilp for dissolving Powder Colors. Glossing for Wax Work. Poonah Brushes. Poonah Badger Brushes. Camels' Hair Quill Brushes. Camels' Hair Pencils in tin. Red Sable Hair Pencils. Arrow Root, pure Bermuda and Taylor's. China Saucers and Slants for mixing Colors. Glass Balls for Currants and Grapes.

WOODEN MOULDING TOOLS and STEEL CURLING PINS.

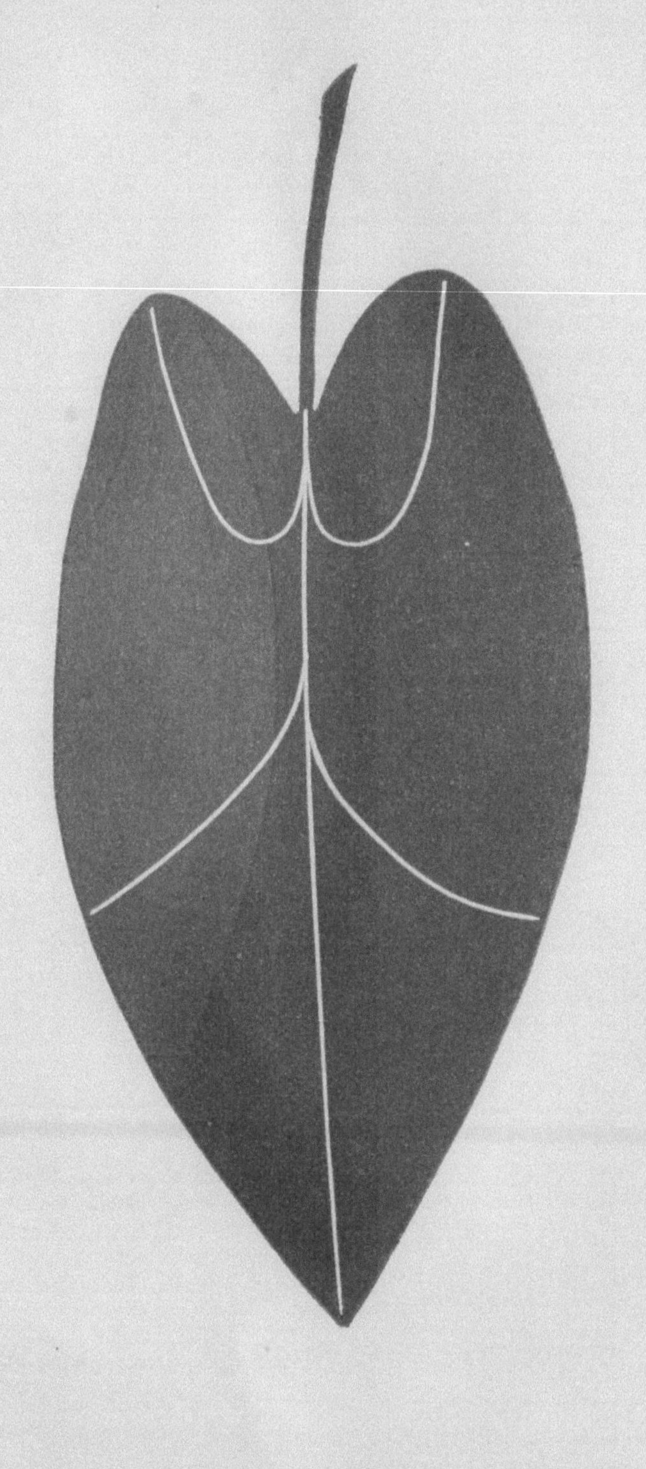

THE ART

OF

Making Wax Leaves,

BY

MRS. A. M. HYDE.

PUBLISHED BY

JANENTZKY & CO., 1125 CHESTNUT STREET,

PHILADELPHIA.

WORKS ON ART.

	EACH.
AUDSLEY, Illuminating,...	$1 50
ALLEN, Young Mechanics' Instructor, or Workmans' Guide,	1 15
BACON, Theory of Colors,..	1 50
BAIGENT, Heraldic Illuminating,....................................	3 00
BARNARD, Foreground Studies,......................................	10 00
BARNARD, Water Color Painting,....................................	8 00
BOUTELL, Heraldry Historical and Popular, Illustrated,.....	9 00
BURNETT, Portrait Painting in Oil Colors,...........	7 50
BARBER, Painters, Grainers, and Writers' Assistant,..........	90
CHAPMAN, American Drawing Book,................................	6 00
CHASE'S Landscape Painting, ...	1 50
CHEVREUIL, on Colors, colored plates,.................	3 00
DELAMOTTE, Primer of Illumination,................................	4 00
FAU'S ANATOMY, with Atlas, plain, $13 50, colored,.......	22 50
FIELDING, Mixed tints and their uses,............................	1 25
GREEN, Perspective,..	6 00
HARDING, Early Drawing Book,.................	5 00
" New Drawing Book,..........	10 00
" Lesions on Trees, and on Art,...	7 50
" Guide and Companion,..	6 00
" Elementary Art,......	12 50
HARRISON, Suggestions for Illuminators,..........................	5 00
MINTORN, Wax Flower Modelling,...................................	1 50
PEPPER, Art of Making Wax Flowers,.............. ...	75
RINTOUL, Painting Photograph Portraits,................	1 25
REINELL, Carpenters, Joiners, and Gilders' Companion,......	67
REINELL, Masons, Bricklayers, Plasterers & Slaters' Assistant	67
TILTON, Wax Flowers and how to make,..............	2 00
" Art Recreation,...	3 00
" Skeleton Leaves,..	2 00
THOMAS, Mural Decoration,..	7 50
WALL, Photograph Painting,.......	3 50
WALKER, Lessons on Animals and Figures,........................	3 75

HAND-BOOKS ON ART.

Per Copy 45 cts. Postage paid 50 cts.

Landscape Painting, in Oil Colors.
Portrait Painting in Oil Colors.
Marine Painting in Oil Colors.
Guide to Oil Painting, Part I. and II.
On the materials used in painting, cleaning and restoring [Oil Paintings.
Landscape Painting in Water Colors.
Portrait Painting in Water Colors.
System of Water Color Painting.
Art of Miniature Painting.
Sketching in Water Colors from Nature.
Guide to Water Color Painting.
Guide to Miniature Painting.
Sketching Trees from N. ture in Water Colors.
A manual of Illumination.
A companion to Guide of Illumination.
Marine Painting in Water Colors.
Principles of Coloring in Painting.
Art of Flower Painting.
Guide to Flower Painting.
Art of mural decoration.
How to Sketch from Nature.
What to Sketch with.
Hand-book of Alphabets.
Hand-book of Initial Letters.
Alphabet and Designs of different periods.
Animal Drawing, by Gullick.
Animal Drawing, by Weigall.
Artistic Anatomy of the Horse.
Artistic Anatomy of the Human Figure.
Transparency Painting on Linen.
Transparency Painting on Glass.
Art of Sketching from Nature.
Elements of Perspective.
Principles of Form in Ornamental Art.
Drawing Models and their uses.
Painting and Drawing in Colored Crayons.
Guide to Light and Shade Drawing.
Guide to Pencil and Chalk Drawing.
Guide to Pictorial Art.
Guide to Levelling and Surveying.
Guide to Pictorial Perspective.
The Art of Figure Drawing, by Weigall.
Guide to Figure Drawing, by Hicks.
Guide to Painting on Glass.

Paraire Perspective.
Art of Wood Engraving.
Painting on Glass for Magic Lantern.
Water Color Painting and Sketching from Nature.
Figure Painting in Water Colors, by Whiteford.
Miniature Painting in Oil and Water Colors.

www.ingramcontent.com/pod-product-compliance
Ingram Content Group UK Ltd.
Pitfield, Milton Keynes, MK11 3LW, UK
UKHW041902190726
13854UKWH00003B/1033